ALL ABOUT ME

My name is _______________

I am from _______________

This is a picture of me!

My birthday is on

____

I am_________ years old.

I live in _______________

This is a picture of my family

My favorite color is

____

My favorite animal is

____

My favorite subject is

____

My favorite food is

____

My favorite sport is

____

Thank You!

Dear Customer,

Thank you so much for your recent purchase of the "500+ Anxiety Solution Affirmations" book. Your support means a lot to us.

We believe that these affirmations will serve as a powerful tool in your journey towards mental wellness. Each affirmation has been carefully crafted with the intention of fostering positivity and resilience in the face of anxiety.

Remember, change takes time and consistency is key. We encourage you to use these affirmations daily and observe the transformation they bring about in your life.

Once again, thank you for your purchase. We are confident that you will find value in our product and we look forward to serving you again in the future.

Best Regards,

Debabrata naik

Copyright

- **I am choosing to embrace my journey with grace and patience.**
- **I trust the wisdom of my inner self.**
- **I am choosing to embrace the power of forgiveness.**
- **I am a beacon of hope and positivity.**
- **I am learning to let go of the fear of criticism.**

- **I am learning to love and accept myself unconditionally.**
- **I am a beacon of light, dispelling darkness with my inner radiance.**
- **I am a source of calm in times of chaos.**
- **I am learning to let go of the fear of loss.**
- **I am choosing to replace fear with love.**

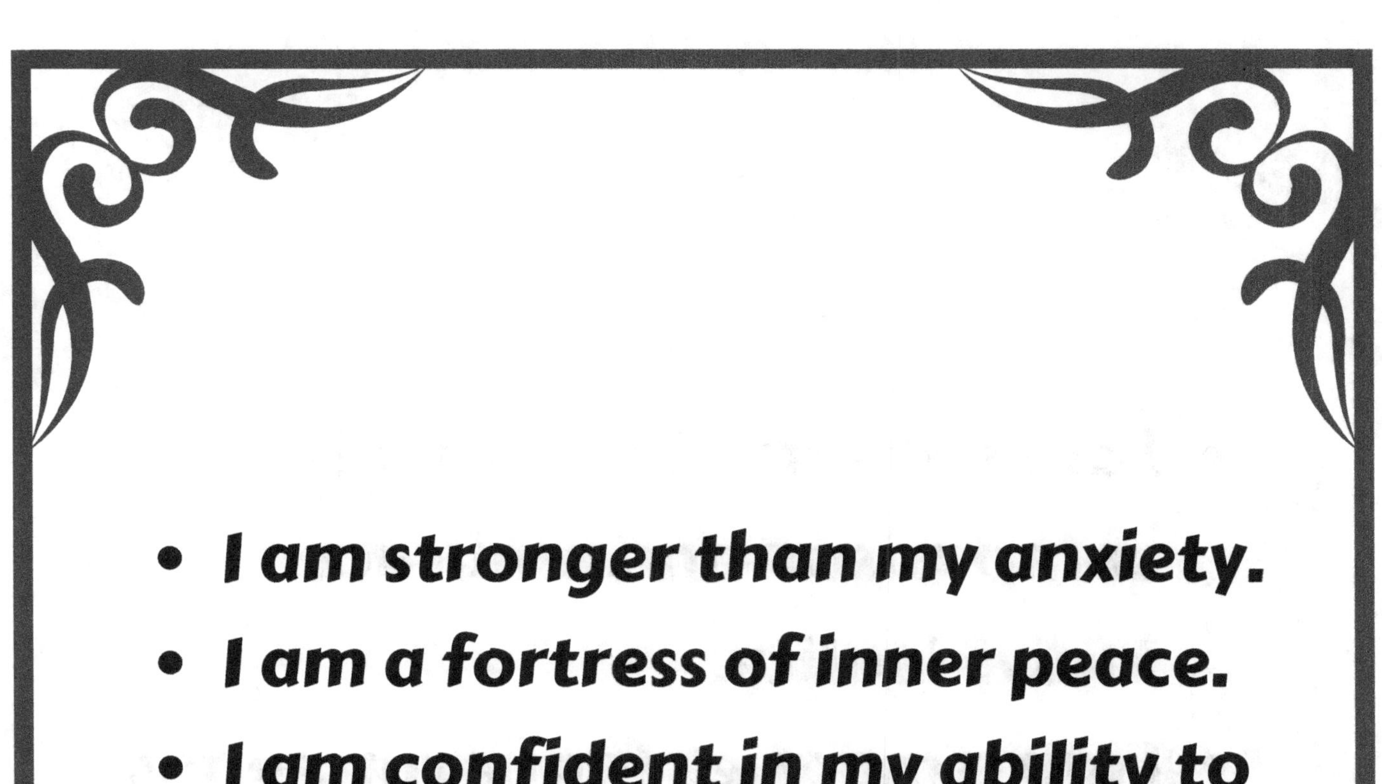

- I am stronger than my anxiety.
- I am a fortress of inner peace.
- I am confident in my ability to surmount any challenge with ease.
- I am in control of my mind, and I choose calmness.
- I am choosing to live a life of freedom and authenticity.

- **I am learning to let go of comparison and embrace individuality.**
- **I am a magnet for harmonious relationships and connections.**
- **I am choosing to celebrate my small victories.**
- **I am a warrior of light, dispelling darkness with love.**
- **I am finding strength in my struggles.**

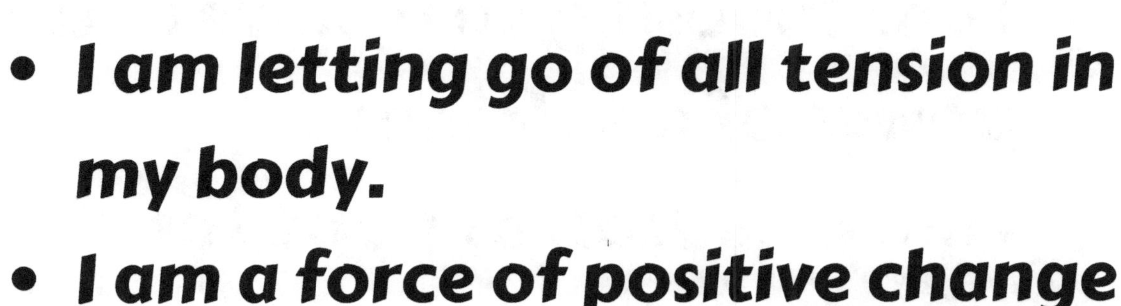

- *I am letting go of all tension in my body.*
- *I am a force of positive change in my own life.*
- *I am free from the burden of anxiety.*
- *I am choosing to focus on my personal development.*
- *I am learning to let go of fear and embrace love.*

- *I am choosing to believe in the power of my dreams.*
- *I am a beacon of hope for myself and others.*
- *I am detaching from worry and attaching to peace.*
- *I am a lighthouse, guiding others to safety with my inner light.*
- *I am embracing the rhythm of my own journey.*

- I am choosing to see the silver lining in every situation.
- I am a channel for peace to flow through me and into the world.
- I am learning to let go of the fear of making mistakes.
- I am a source of hope, joy, and positivity for myself and others.
- I am choosing to focus on my inner strength.

- **I am choosing to live a life of joy and contentment.**
- **I am calm and composed in the face of life's challenges.**
- **I am choosing to embrace the power of self-discovery.**
- **I am as steadfast as a mountain in the face of adversity.**
- **I am learning to let go of the need for perfection.**

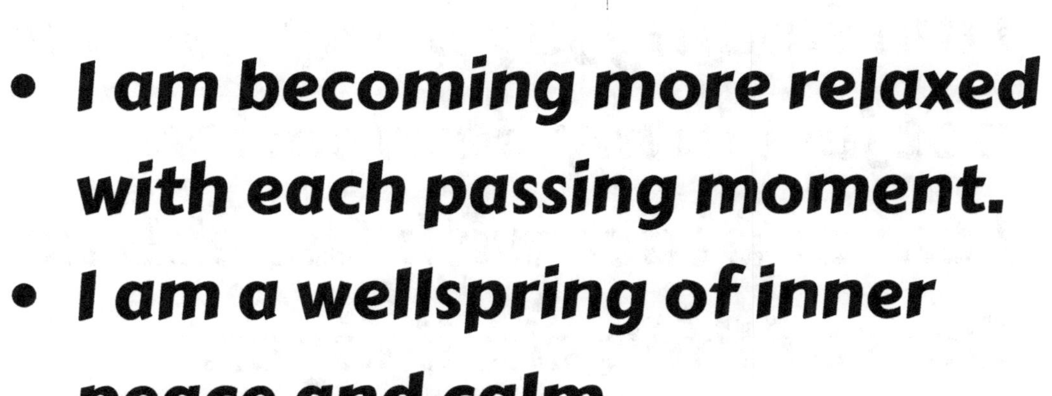

- **I am becoming more relaxed with each passing moment.**
- **I am a wellspring of inner peace and calm.**
- **I am learning to trust in the power of my intuition.**
- **I am a reservoir of inner strength and resilience.**
- **I am choosing to embrace self-understanding.**

- **I am finding joy in my journey, not just in my destination.**
- **I am at peace with the ebb and flow of life's challenges.**
- **I am focusing on my personal growth and self-improvement.**
- **I am confident in my ability to handle whatever comes my way.**
- **I am learning to let go of the fear of vulnerability.**

- I am learning to let go of past hurts and forgive those who have wronged me.
- I am a vessel of calm in the midst of chaos.
- I am learning to let go of the need for validation.
- I am a source of joy and laughter.
- I am choosing to focus on my inner understanding.

- I am learning to let go of fear and embrace courage.
- I am a channel for peace and tranquility to flow through me.
- I am free of worry and am at peace with who I am.
- I am deserving of love, happiness, and peace.
- I am learning to be my own best friend.

- **I am releasing negative thoughts and welcoming serenity.**
- **I am a source of comfort and strength for myself and others.**
- **I am learning to trust in the power of my own journey.**
- **I am a resilient and adaptable soul.**
- **I am more than capable of conquering my fears.**

- I am learning to let go of the fear of not being good enough.
- I am grateful for the peace and tranquility in my life.
- I am choosing to focus on my spiritual growth.
- I am a magnet for positive experiences.
- I am learning to let go of the fear of loneliness.

- I am choosing to embrace the power of self-realization.
- I am a beacon of serenity in a chaotic world.
- I am transforming my challenges into opportunities.
- I am free from the grip of anxious thoughts.
- I am finding joy in the present moment.

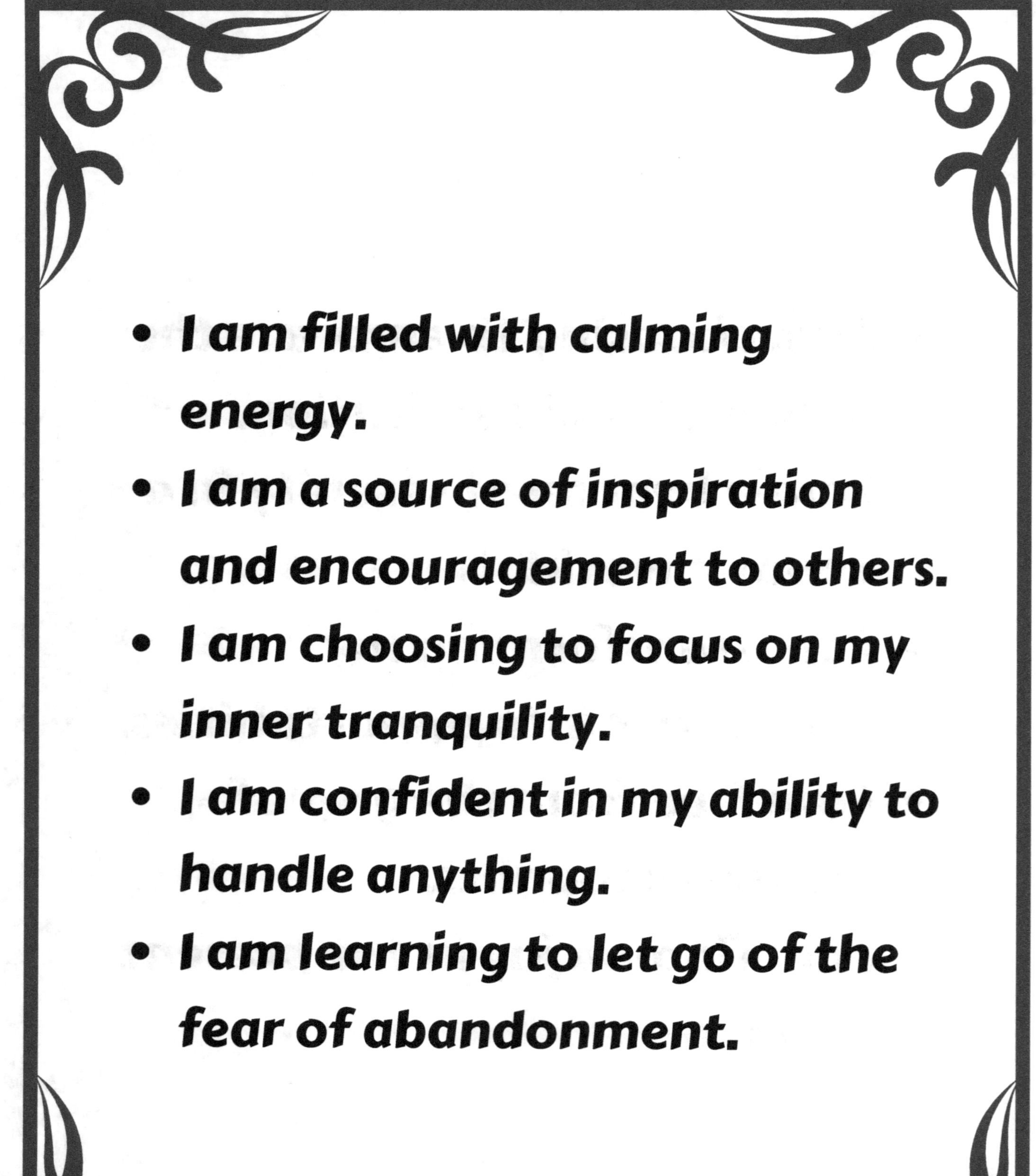

- I am filled with calming energy.
- I am a source of inspiration and encouragement to others.
- I am choosing to focus on my inner tranquility.
- I am confident in my ability to handle anything.
- I am learning to let go of the fear of abandonment.

- **I am learning to let go of negativity and embrace positivity.**
- **I am at peace with the present moment.**
- **I am choosing to embrace self-awareness.**
- **I am in charge of my thoughts, and I choose positivity.**
- **I am learning to let go of the fear of being judged.**

- I am grateful for the strength that helps me overcome my fears.
- I am in control of my thoughts and emotions, and I choose tranquility.
- I am choosing to embrace self-empowerment.
- I am a vessel of love and compassion.
- I am a warrior, not a worrier.

- **I am choosing to create my own path and follow my own journey.**

- **I am at peace with my past, present, and future.**

- **I am choosing to embrace the power of self-fulfillment.**

- **I am a magnet for positive energy and good vibes.**

- **I am learning to trust in the power of my own voice.**

- **I am learning to let go of the need for constant achievement.**
- **I am confident in my ability to navigate life's twists and turns.**
- **I am choosing to see the world with love and kindness.**
- **I am in harmony with the cosmic symphony of existence.**
- **I am learning to be patient with myself on my journey.**

- **I am choosing to embrace the power of self-compassion.**
- **I am a warrior of light, dispelling darkness with my inner radiance.**
- **I am choosing to live a life of abundance and prosperity.**
- **I am in control of my inner world and emotions.**
- **I am resilient and can get through anything.**

- **I am grounded in the experience of the present moment.**
- **I am a master of my thoughts and emotions.**
- **I am learning to let go of the need for achievement.**
- **I am a sanctuary of love and positivity.**
- **I am confident in my ability to solve problems.**

- I am cultivating a peaceful mind.
- I am a beacon of hope for those around me.
- I am safe and everything is good in my world.
- I am a source of inspiration and empowerment.
- I am attracting positive energy into my body.

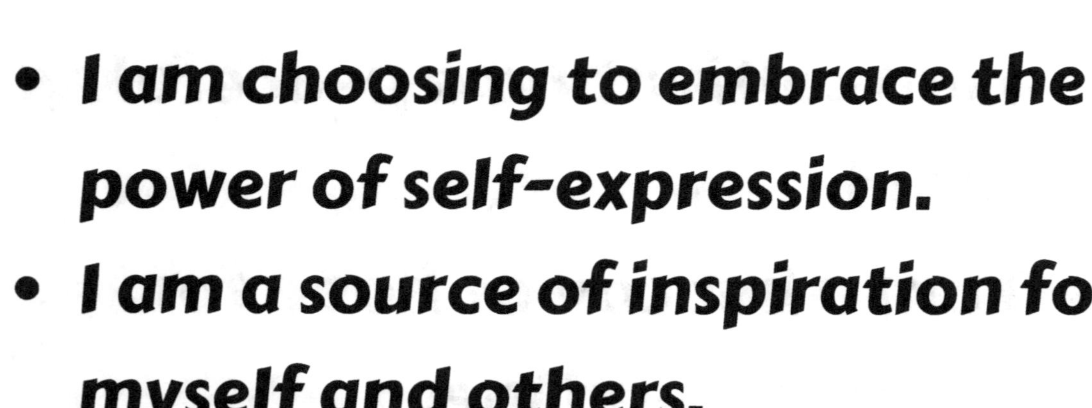

- I am choosing to embrace the power of self-expression.
- I am a source of inspiration for myself and others.
- I am letting go of all that no longer serves my growth.
- I am adaptable, flexible, and open to change.
- I am choosing to embrace the power of self-confidence.

- **I am learning to trust the journey, even when I do not understand it.**
- **I am a conduit for positive change in my life.**
- **I am learning to see the beauty in every moment.**
- **I am at peace with myself and the world.**
- **I am choosing to love myself just as I am.**

- I am focusing on my journey, not the destination.
- I am capable of handling uncertainty with grace and courage.
- I am choosing to believe in my dreams.
- I am at ease with uncertainty.
- I am choosing to embrace the power of self-worth.

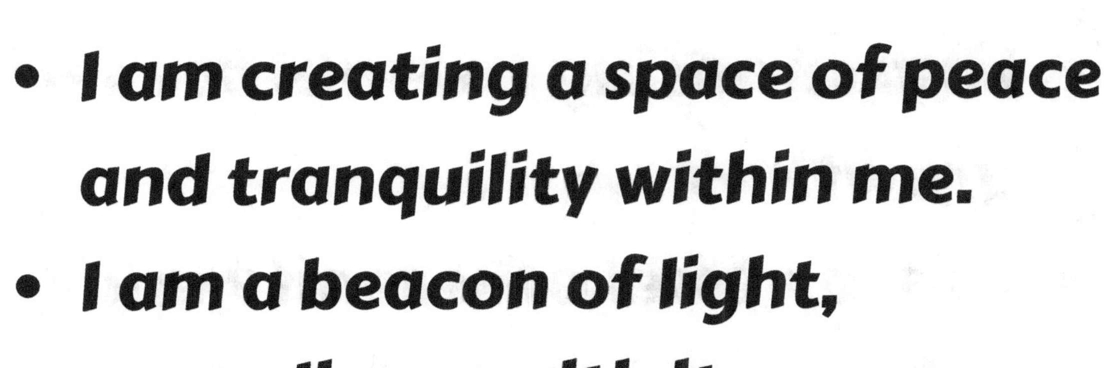

- **I am creating a space of peace and tranquility within me.**
- **I am a beacon of light, spreading positivity.**
- **I am choosing to release all negative thoughts.**
- **I am a reservoir of inner strength.**
- **I am confident in overcoming my fears.**

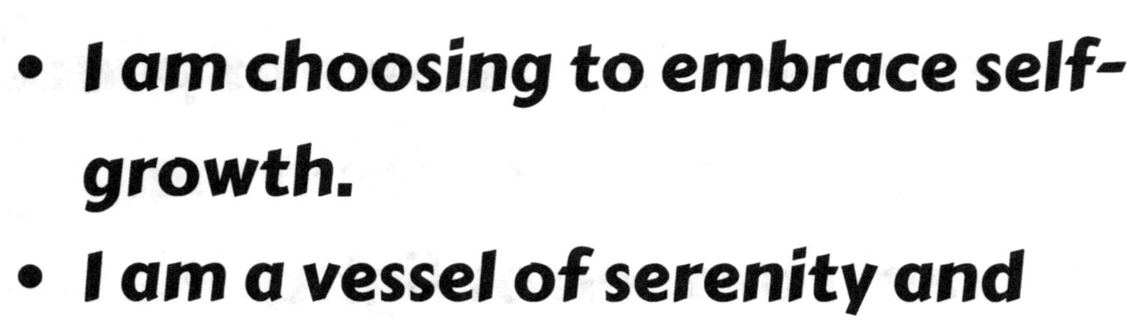

- I am choosing to embrace self-growth.
- I am a vessel of serenity and calmness.
- I am choosing to focus on the positive.
- I am confident in my ability to face challenges head-on.
- I am at peace with my past, present, and future.

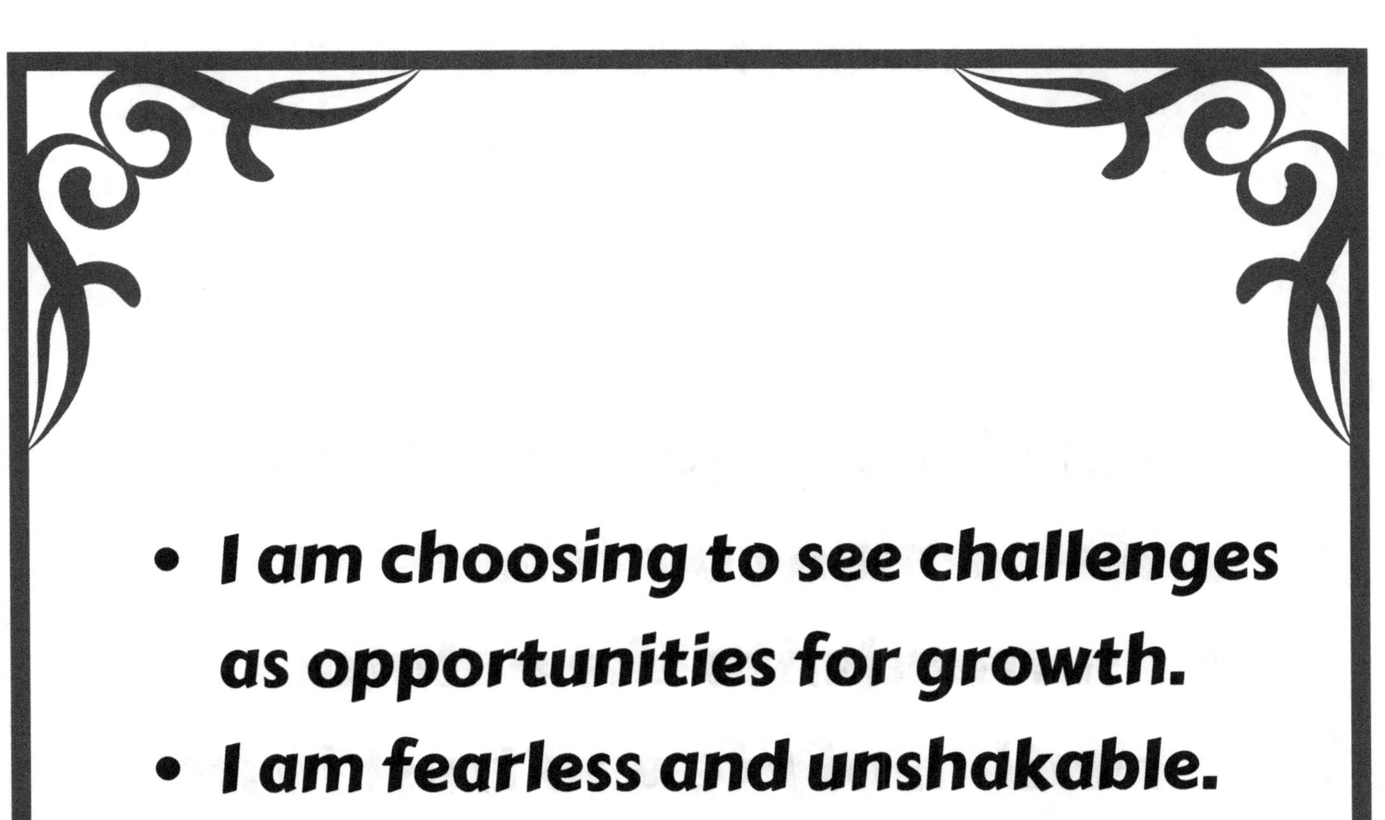

- **I am choosing to see challenges as opportunities for growth.**
- **I am fearless and unshakable.**
- **I am choosing to nourish my mind with positive thoughts.**
- **I am a magnet for positive energy.**
- **I am surrounded by love and positivity.**

- I am letting go of fear and welcoming comfort.
- I surrender to the natural rhythm of life and trust in its intelligence.
- I am choosing to focus on my peace of mind.
- I trust the process of life and let go of resistance.
- I am choosing to embrace self-discovery.

- I am choosing to live a life of creativity and inspiration.
- I am open to the healing power of relaxation.
- I am choosing to focus on my emotional health.
- I am open to new opportunities and adventures.
- I am choosing to embrace self-realization.

- I am learning to let go of the need for external validation.
- I am in sync with the natural flow of life.
- I am learning to embrace the unknown and trust in the process.
- I am open to the blessings of each day.
- I am discovering new ways to reduce my anxiety.

- I am learning to let go of what I cannot control and focus on what I can.
- I trust in the unfolding of my journey.
- I am learning to let go of guilt and regret.
- I release anxiety and invite joy into my life.
- I am learning to appreciate every step of my journey.

- I am growing stronger with every breath.
- I surrender to the natural flow of life and trust in its wisdom.
- I am filled with tranquility and harmony.
- I release all tension and welcome relaxation into my body.
- I am choosing to be kind to myself today.

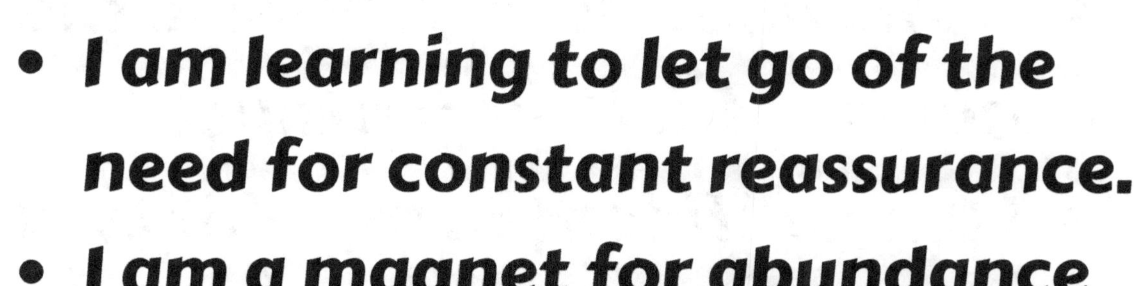

- **I am learning to let go of the need for constant reassurance.**
- **I am a magnet for abundance and prosperity.**
- **I am learning to accept myself, flaws and all.**
- **I am a vessel of kindness and understanding.**
- **I am not defined by my anxiety.**

- I am choosing to embrace the power of self-acceptance.
- I am confident in my ability to adapt and thrive in any circumstance.
- I am learning to let go of fear of the unknown.
- I am fearless and courageous in the face of challenges.
- I am cultivating patience to overcome anxiety.

- **I am learning to trust in the power of love and compassion.**
- **I am in harmony with the rhythm of life.**
- **I am learning to trust in the power of love and kindness.**
- **I am resilient like a phoenix, rising from the ashes.**
- **I am learning to let go of limiting beliefs.**

- I am choosing to be brave in the face of adversity.
- I am strong, capable, and resilient, like a mighty oak tree.
- I am finding peace in every breath.
- I am the master of my thoughts and emotions.
- I am choosing to believe in my abilities and strengths.

- **I am embracing all the possibilities of my future.**
- **I am a beacon of hope for those around me.**
- **I am learning to let go of the need for constant success.**
- **I am in control of my thoughts, and I choose joy and happiness.**
- **I am choosing to see the good in every situation.**

- **I am learning to let go of the need to please everyone.**
- **I am open to receiving abundance and prosperity in all aspects of life.**
- **I am choosing to focus on my mental health.**
- **I am open to the beauty of the present moment.**
- **I am learning to trust in my inner wisdom.**

- **I am choosing to be grateful for my journey and all it has taught me.**
- **I am a source of positivity and hope.**
- **I am choosing to live a life of courage and resilience.**
- **I am calm, confident, and capable.**
- **I am living in this moment and this moment only.**

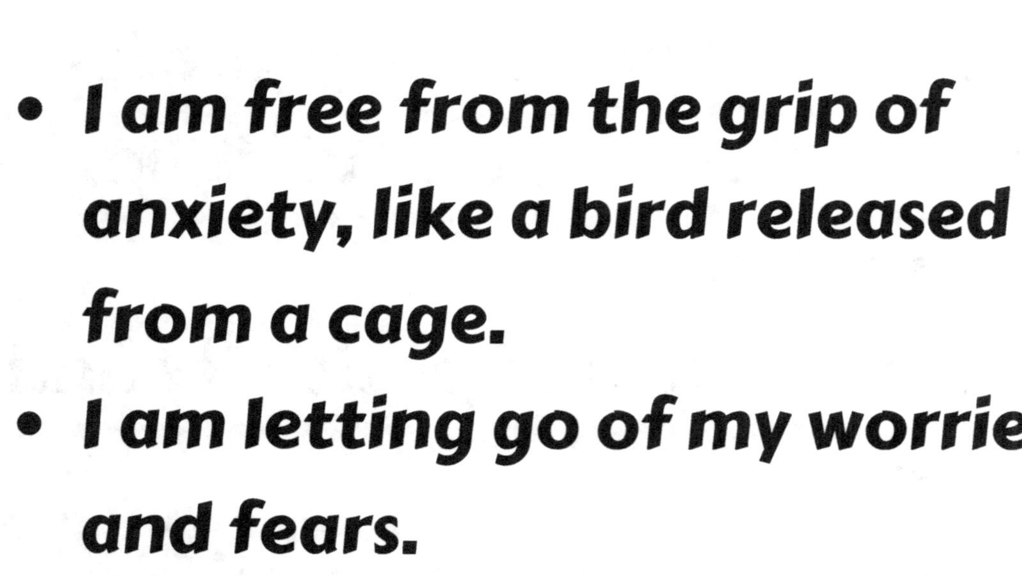

- I am free from the grip of anxiety, like a bird released from a cage.
- I am letting go of my worries and fears.
- I am open to receiving the abundance of the universe.
- I am learning to be gentle with myself.
- I am trusting in my abilities.

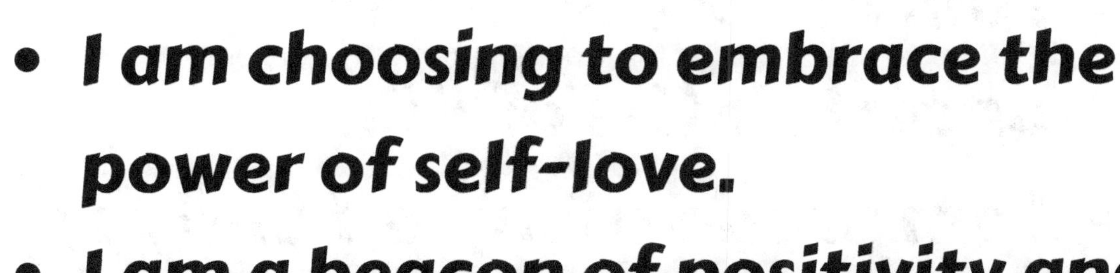

- **I am choosing to embrace the power of self-love.**
- **I am a beacon of positivity and hope.**
- **I am brave and not afraid to keep going.**
- **I am surrounded by peace and love.**
- **I am a vessel of calm and peace.**

- I am at ease with the uncertainties of life.
- I am proud of myself and my accomplishments.
- I am confident, self-assured, and unshakable in my resolve.
- I am learning to see beauty in the small moments.
- I am choosing to see each day as a new opportunity for growth.

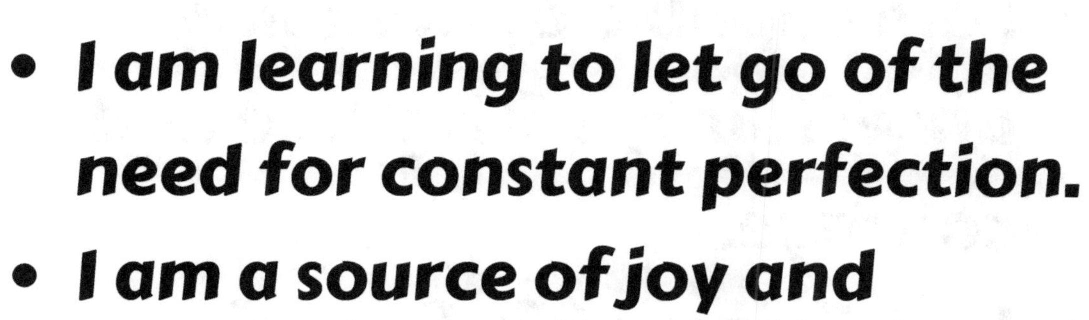

- **I am learning to let go of the need for constant perfection.**
- **I am a source of joy and positivity.**
- **I am embracing the journey towards inner peace.**
- **I am a beacon of positivity and light.**
- **I am in control of my thoughts and my life.**

- I am capable of handling uncertainty with grace and courage.
- I am living a life free of anxiety.
- I am centered and grounded in the present moment.
- I am trusting in my journey and the path I am on.
- I am confident and self-assured in my decisions.

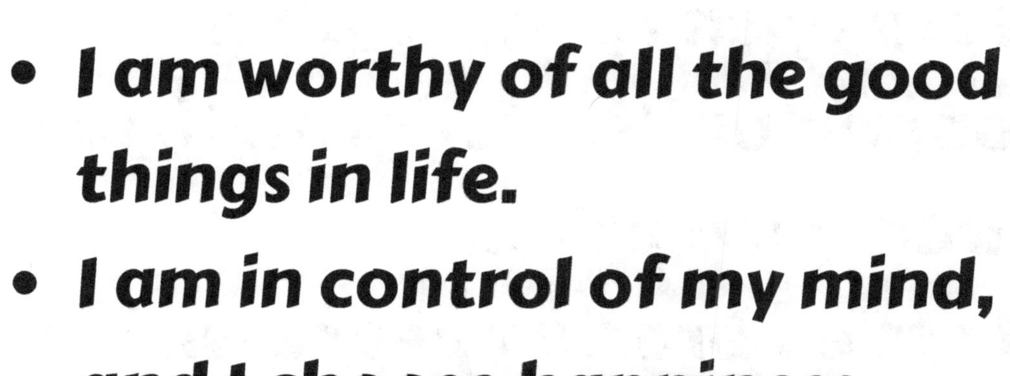

- **I am worthy of all the good things in life.**
- **I am in control of my mind, and I choose happiness.**
- **I am learning to trust in the power of my dreams and aspirations.**
- **I am at ease with uncertainty.**
- **I am choosing to live a life of peace and serenity.**

- **I am open to the endless opportunities for growth and transformation.**
- **I am embracing peace within me.**
- **I am resilient and can adapt to any circumstance.**
- **I am letting go of all fear and doubt.**
- **I choose to focus on the present moment.**

- I am choosing to honor my feelings and emotions.
- I am the architect of my own happiness.
- I am learning to let go of the fear of judgment.
- I am open to the wisdom of my intuition.
- I am choosing to practice mindfulness daily.

- I release all anxiety and tension from my body.
- I am letting go of all fear and embracing faith.
- I release all negative energy from my body and mind.
- I am welcoming serenity into my heart.
- I surrender to the natural flow of life.

- **I am learning to let go of judgment and embrace acceptance.**
- **I am in control of my reactions and responses.**
- **I am choosing to live a life of balance and harmony.**
- **I am resilient and adaptable.**
- **I am learning to trust in my own abilities.**

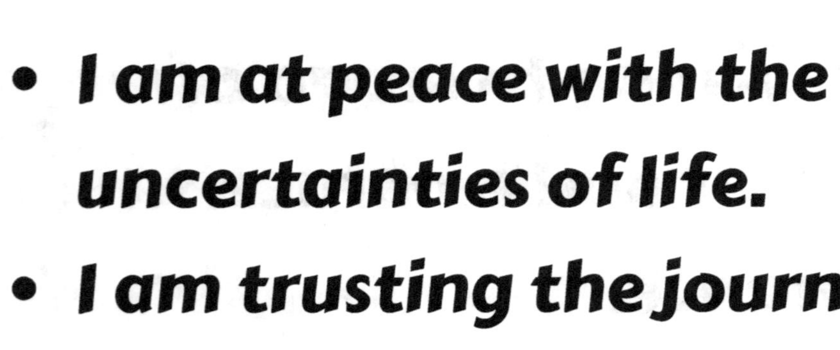

- *I am at peace with the uncertainties of life.*
- *I am trusting the journey of my life.*
- *I am calm and composed in every situation.*
- *I am choosing to focus on my healing.*
- *I am confident in my ability to overcome any obstacle.*

- *I am choosing to embrace the power of self-esteem.*
- *I am calm and composed in all situations.*
- *I am focusing on the things I can control.*
- *I am grounded, like the roots of a mighty tree.*
- *I am learning to let go of self-judgment.*

- **I am in harmony with the natural order of the universe.**
- **I am choosing to love myself unconditionally.**
- **I am open to the beauty and wonder of each day.**
- **I am learning to let go of the need for approval.**
- **I am safe, and I trust in the universe's plan for me.**

- I am in control of my emotions and thoughts.
- I am confident in my ability to navigate life's twists and turns.
- I am finding joy in every moment.
- I am deserving of all the blessings that come my way.
- I am becoming more at ease with each breath.

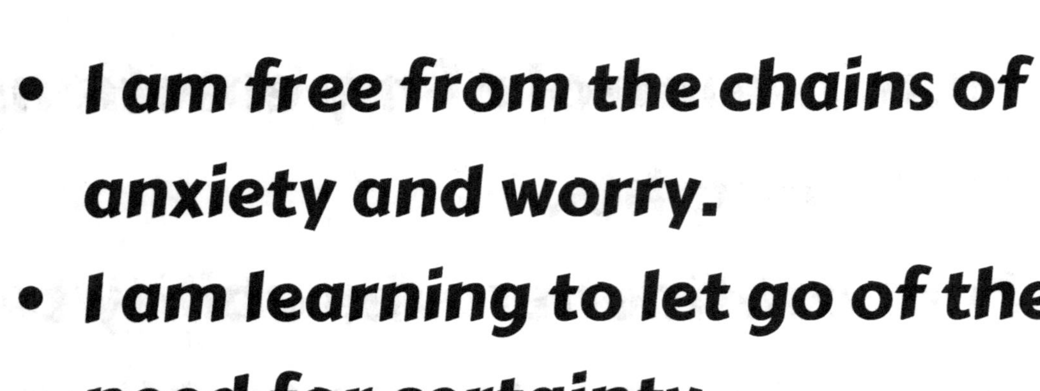

- I am free from the chains of anxiety and worry.
- I am learning to let go of the need for certainty.
- I am in control of my responses to life's challenges.
- I am choosing to embrace self-respect.
- I trust that everything happens for my highest good.

- **I am learning to let go of the need for recognition.**
- **I am deserving of all the good things that come my way.**
- **I am learning to let go of the need for control.**
- **I am free from the grip of anxiety and worry.**
- **I am choosing to embrace self-compassion.**

- I am in control of my inner peace, and I choose tranquility.
- I am choosing to focus on positivity.
- I am in charge of my thoughts, and I choose optimism.
- I am choosing to embrace self-esteem.
- I am in harmony with the natural flow of life.

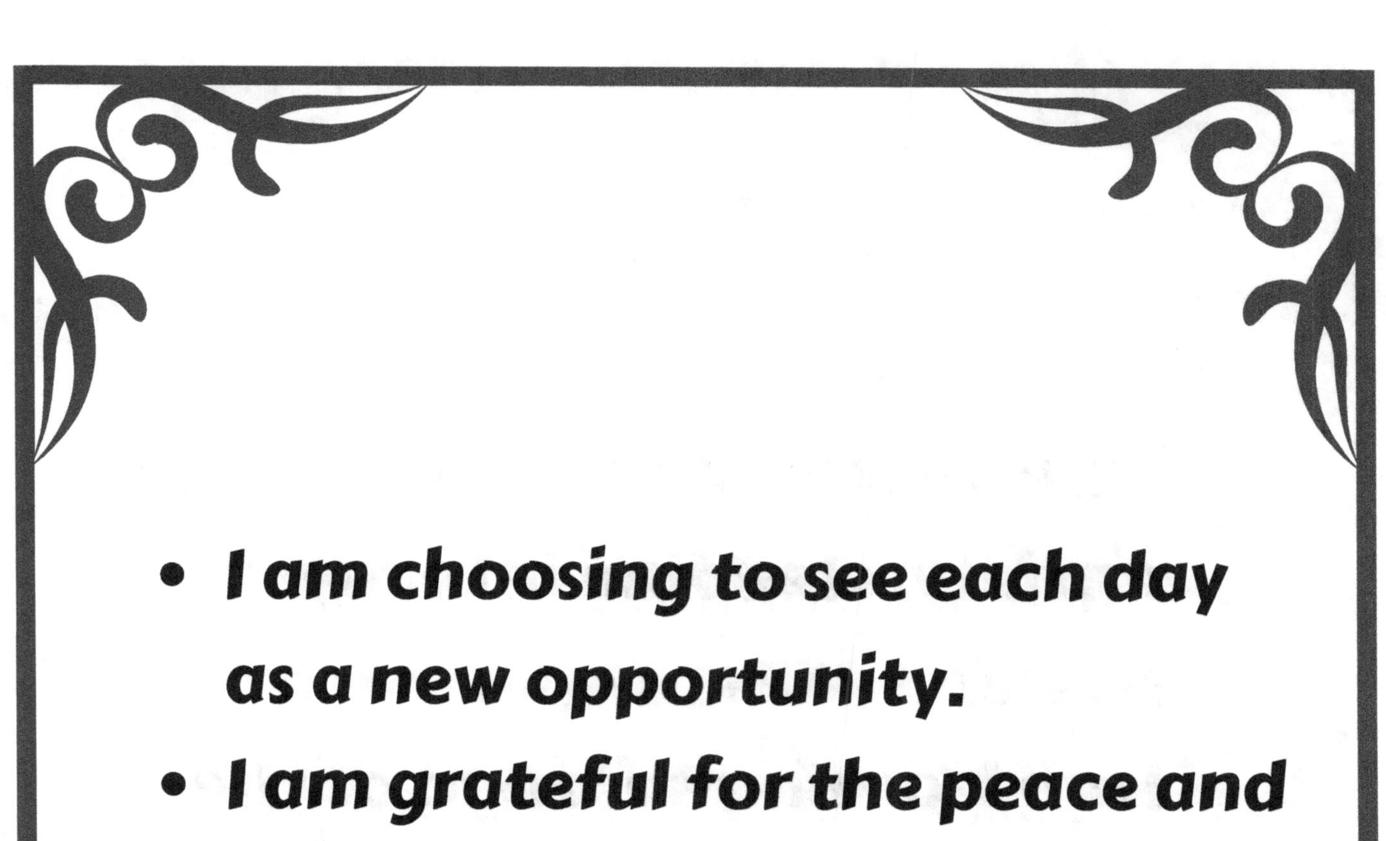

- I am choosing to see each day as a new opportunity.
- I am grateful for the peace and stillness within.
- I am choosing to be grateful for all that I have.
- I am fearless and courageous.
- I am trusting in the process of life.

- I am liberated from the grip of anxiety, stepping into my power.
- I am learning to let go of the need to be right.
- I am open to the endless possibilities that life offers.
- I am choosing to see challenges as opportunities.
- I am safe and protected at all times.

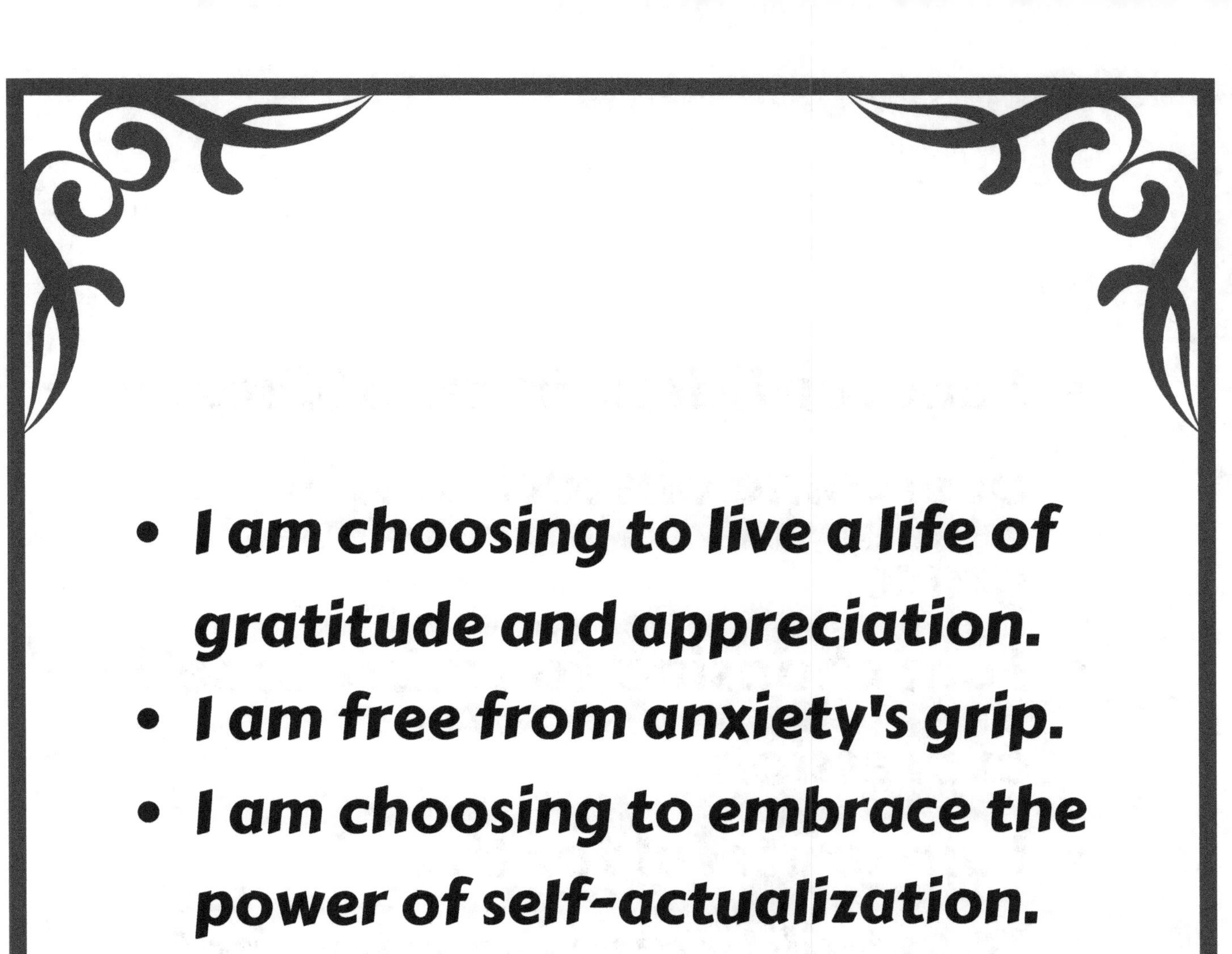

- **I am choosing to live a life of gratitude and appreciation.**
- **I am free from anxiety's grip.**
- **I am choosing to embrace the power of self-actualization.**
- **I am fearless and resolute in pursuing my dreams.**
- **I am learning to let go of the fear of conflict.**

- I am confident in my ability to overcome obstacles with grace.
- I am choosing to embrace self-expression.
- I am grateful for the tranquility and serenity that fills my life.
- I am choosing to live a life of health and wellness.
- I am in control of my thoughts, and I choose positivity.

- **I am learning to let go of the need for material possessions.**
- **I am grounded and centered in the present moment.**
- **I am choosing to live in alignment with my values.**
- **I am free from the shackles of fear and worry.**
- **I am learning to let go of comparison.**

- I am grateful for the lessons that anxiety has taught me.
- I am choosing to create my own happiness.
- I am in control of my thoughts and emotions, choosing peace and tranquility.
- I am learning to replace worry with hope.
- I am present and fully engaged in each moment.

- I am releasing all worries from my mind.
- I am in harmony with the universe.
- I am choosing to embrace self-actualization.
- I am free from the chains of anxiety, like a butterfly breaking free from its cocoon.
- I am letting go of today's stress.

- I am in control of my thoughts, and I choose positivity and optimism.
- I am learning to trust in the journey of life.
- I am open to receiving the blessings of the universe in abundance.
- I am choosing to focus on my personal growth.
- I am open to the endless possibilities that life presents.

- I am choosing to embrace the power of self-belief.
- I am grateful for the serenity in my life.
- I am replacing worry with action.
- I am strong, capable, and adaptable.
- I am learning to let go of the fear of uncertainty.

- I am safe and protected by the loving energy of the cosmos.
- I am focusing on positive progress.
- I let go of all tension and stress, allowing my body to relax completely.
- I am choosing to live in the present moment.
- I trust in my ability to handle whatever comes my way.

- I am choosing to live in alignment with my highest values.
- I trust in my capacity to handle life's challenges with grace.
- I am learning to embrace my unique journey and path.
- I surrender to the flow of life and trust in its wisdom
- I am calm, patient, and in control of my emotions.

- I release the need for external validation and find validation within myself.
- I am transforming my fear into courage.
- I let go of the past and embrace the limitless possibilities of the future.
- I am embracing the power of positivity.
- I radiate love, peace, and positivity.

- **I am learning to be patient with myself and my journey.**
- **I am free from the grip of fear and doubt.**
- **I am choosing to let go of perfectionism.**
- **I am in control of my thoughts and emotions.**
- **I am learning to let go of the fear of disappointment.**

- **I am open to receiving all the abundance that the universe has to offer.**

- **I am open to all the healing life has to offer.**

- **I am present in the here and now, fully engaged with life's beauty.**

- **I am choosing to focus on my happiness.**

- **I am safe, and the universe is on my side.**

- **I am learning to love and accept myself just as I am.**
- **I am free from the chains of anxiety.**
- **I am choosing to live a life of passion and purpose.**
- **I am in perfect alignment with the universe.**
- **I am learning to let go of the need for acceptance.**

- I am resilient like a mountain, standing strong in the face of adversity.
- I am choosing to focus on my inner harmony.
- I let go of the need to control everything and allow life to unfold naturally.
- I am learning to embrace change.
- I trust in the unfolding of my life's journey.

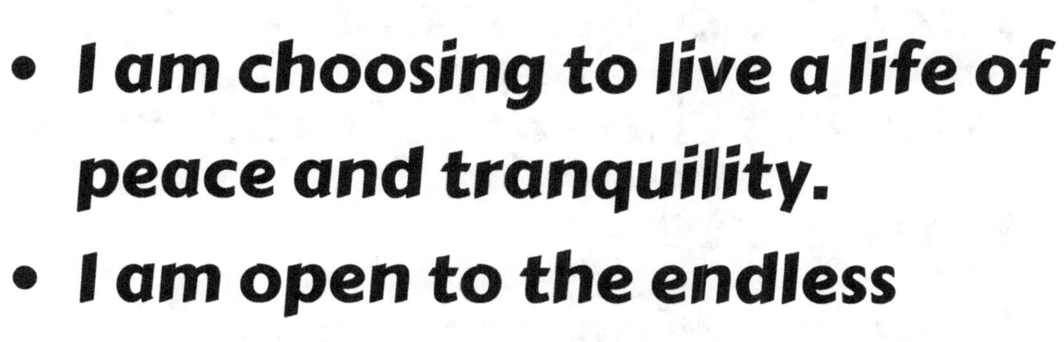

- I am choosing to live a life of peace and tranquility.
- I am open to the endless possibilities of life.
- I am choosing to live a life of love and compassion.
- I am surrounded by love and support.
- I am letting go of all that does not serve me.

- I am the captain of my ship, steering through stormy seas with grace.
- I am learning to let go of resentment.
- I let go of all resistance and flow with the river of life.
- I am learning to let go of the fear of rejection.
- I release all fear and doubt from my mind.

- **I am capable of handling whatever comes my way.**
- **I am in perfect alignment with my true self.**
- **I am finding peace in letting go of expectations.**
- **I am in tune with my body and its needs.**
- **I am choosing to be brave in the face of fear.**

- **I am resilient like a sturdy oak tree, bending but not breaking.**
- **I am choosing to focus on my inner calm.**
- **I let go of all anxiety and tension, allowing my body to relax.**
- **I am learning to trust in the power of my dreams.**
- **I release all self-doubt and embrace self-confidence.**

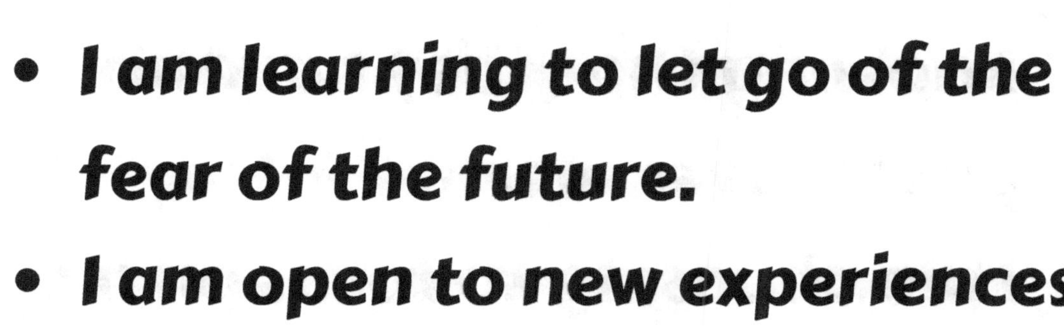

- I am learning to let go of the fear of the future.
- I am open to new experiences and opportunities.
- I am choosing to be kind to myself and others.
- I trust in the process of life's unfolding.
- I am choosing to live a life of joy and happiness.

- **I release all worries and fears, knowing that they have no power over me.**
- **I am choosing to focus on my inner patience.**
- **I breathe deeply and calmly, releasing tension with each breath.**
- **I am choosing to embrace self-fulfillment.**
- **I am worthy of love, happiness, and peace.**

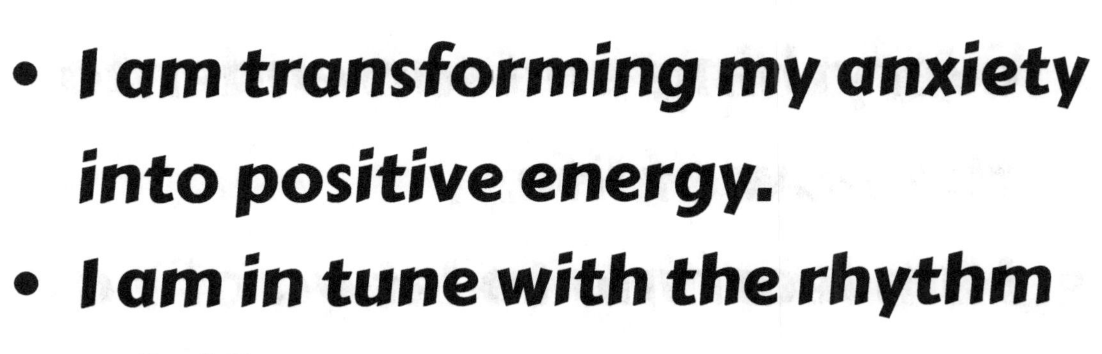

- I am transforming my anxiety into positive energy.
- I am in tune with the rhythm of life.
- I am capable of navigating through my challenges.
- I am resilient like a phoenix, rising from challenges.
- I am learning to embrace change as a part of life.

- I release the need to control everything and surrender to the flow of life.
- I am learning to let go of past hurts and forgive.
- I trust in the unfolding of my path, even when it appears unclear.
- I am finding strength in my vulnerability.
- I let go of judgment and cultivate self-compassion.

- I am choosing to embrace the power of self-trust.
- I am free from the shackles of anxiety.
- I am learning to let go of the fear of inadequacy.
- I am in perfect alignment with the divine order of the universe.
- I am choosing to be resilient in the face of adversity.

- **I am the master of my thoughts, choosing only those that serve my highest good.**
- **I am choosing to focus on my inner serenity.**
- **I release all negative thoughts and replace them with positive ones.**
- **I am choosing to trust in my decisions.**
- **I trust myself to handle any situation that comes my way.**

- **I am learning to let go of the fear of the unknown.**
- **I am in control of my thoughts, and I choose calmness.**
- **I am choosing to live a life of purpose and passion.**
- **I am free from the grip of anxiety.**
- **I am learning to let go of the need for security.**

- I trust the journey of life and let go of the need to control everything.
- I am on a journey towards peace and serenity.
- I release the need for perfection and embrace my imperfections.
- I am choosing to be kind to myself.
- I let go of the need to control every outcome.

- I am embracing the power of positive thinking.
- I am the creator of my own reality.
- I am learning to let go of the need for success.
- I am in control of my thoughts and emotions, and I choose peace.
- I am learning to let go of the need for status.

- **I release all negative thoughts and emotions, creating space for positivity.**
- **I am choosing to embrace self-love.**
- **I am strong, capable, and resilient in the face of adversity.**
- **I am learning to let go of expectations.**
- **I am safe and secure in the embrace of the universe.**

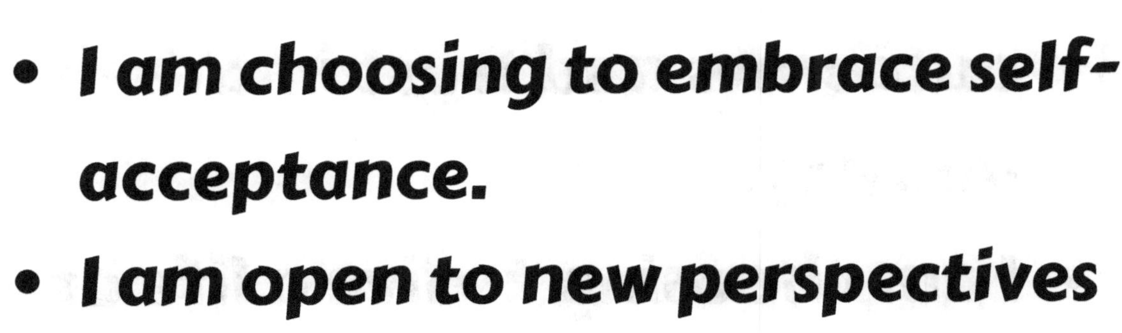

- I am choosing to embrace self-acceptance.
- I am open to new perspectives that bring me peace.
- I am learning to embrace the rhythm of life.
- I am resilient and can bounce back from any setback.
- I am choosing to focus on my inner joy.

- **I release all attachments to outcomes and trust in the journey.**
- **I am choosing to live a life of abundance.**
- **I release any need for external validation and find validation within.**
- **I am learning to embrace change and growth.**
- **I let go of worry and embrace inner peace.**

- **I am safe and protected by the loving energy of the universe.**
- **I am learning to let go of negative self-talk.**
- **I am resilient and can handle anything that comes my way.**
- **I am releasing the need for control.**
- **I release all doubts and embrace unwavering self-belief.**

- I release the need to please others and honor my own needs.

- I am learning to let go of fear of failure.

- I release all worries and fears, knowing they are not my truth.

- I am learning to let go of past mistakes.

- I am safe, and I trust in the process of life.

- I release all negative thoughts and emotions from my being.
- I am finding strength in my calmness.
- I release all worries and fears, knowing they have no power over me.
- I am choosing to embrace self-belief.
- I am worthy of happiness and tranquility.

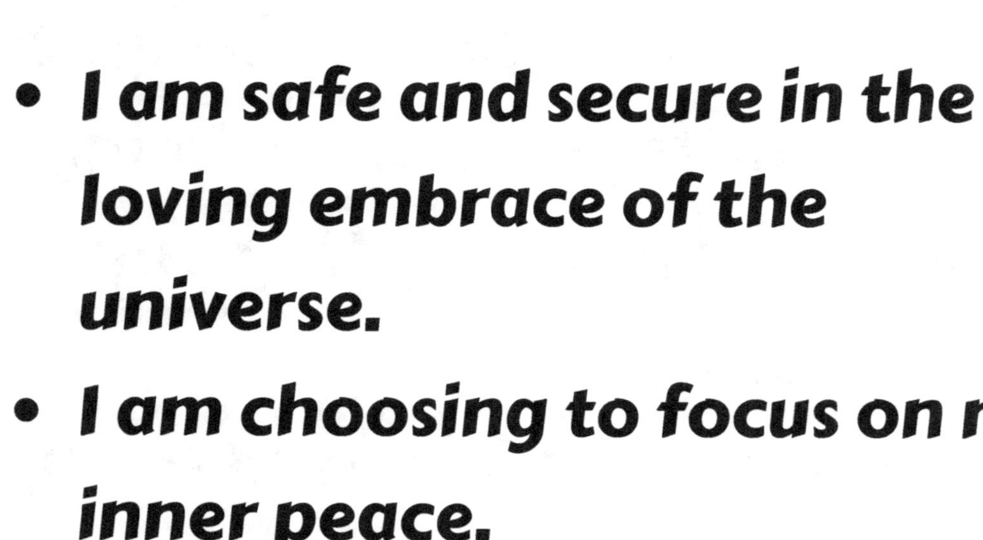

- **I am safe and secure in the loving embrace of the universe.**
- **I am choosing to focus on my inner peace.**
- **I release all worries about the future and live in the present.**
- **I am proud of my progress.**
- **I trust that life unfolds in divine timing.**

- **I am open to receiving abundance in all areas of my life.**
- **I am choosing to focus on my inner resilience.**
- **I am resilient and capable of overcoming challenges.**
- **I am learning to appreciate the journey.**
- **I am worthy of all the blessings in my life.**

- **I release all worries and doubts, making space for serenity.**
- **I am choosing to embrace my uniqueness.**
- **I release the burden of overthinking and find clarity in simplicity.**
- **I am learning to cultivate inner peace.**
- **I trust in the unfolding of my life's story.**

- I release all resistance and flow with the river of life.
- I am choosing to practice self-care regularly.
- I release the past and welcome the present with open arms.
- I am choosing to embrace self-worth.
- I am open to the infinite possibilities that life presents.

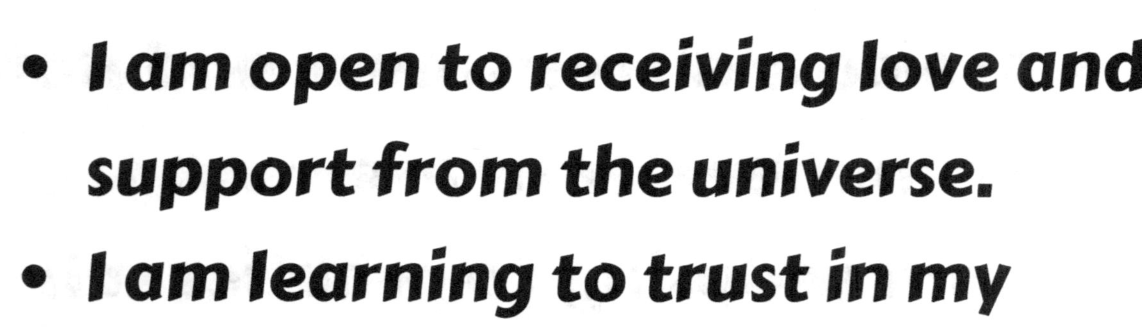

- I am open to receiving love and support from the universe.
- I am learning to trust in my inner strength.
- I release the need for control and embrace the flow of life.
- I am learning to trust in the timing of my life.
- I let go of resistance and accept what is.

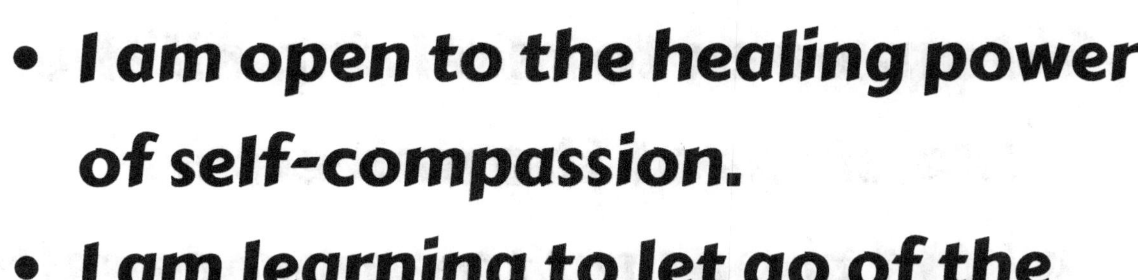

- **I am open to the healing power of self-compassion.**
- **I am learning to let go of the fear of the past.**
- **I release all anxiety, allowing my spirit to soar.**
- **I am learning to be patient with my progress.**
- **I trust in the divine timing of my life.**

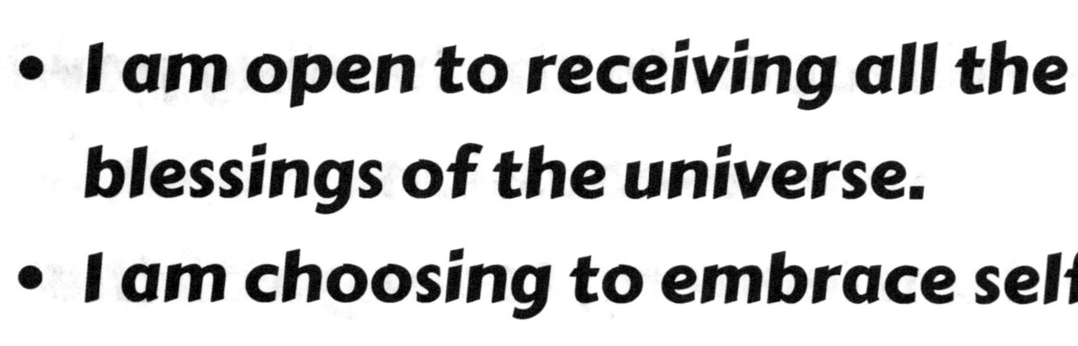

- **I am open to receiving all the blessings of the universe.**
- **I am choosing to embrace self-trust.**
- **I release all negativity from my mind and heart.**
- **I am choosing to focus on my inner balance.**
- **I trust in the divine plan for my life.**

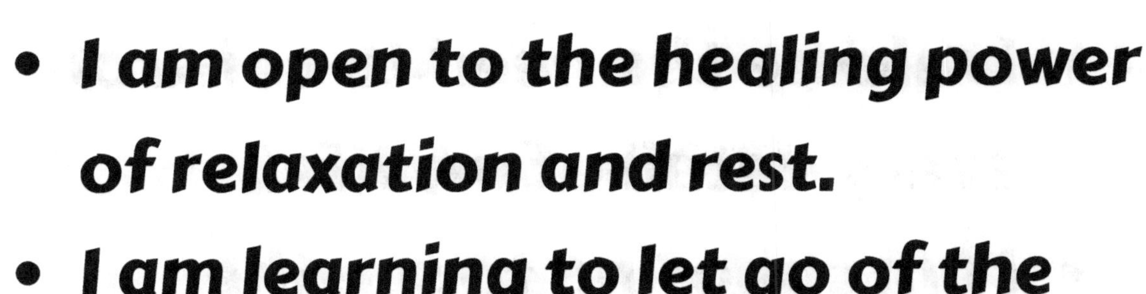

- I am open to the healing power of relaxation and rest.
- I am learning to let go of the need for comfort.
- I release all anxiety from my mind and body.
- I am choosing to focus on my inner courage.
- I release any attachment to fear and embrace love.

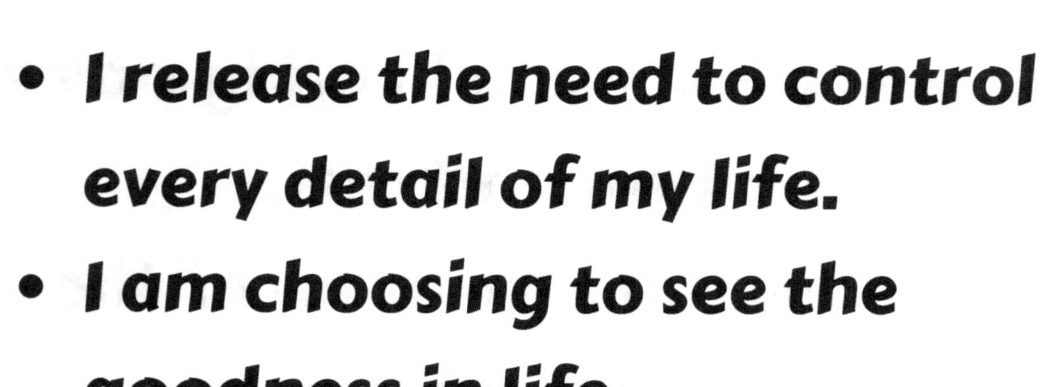

- I release the need to control every detail of my life.
- I am choosing to see the goodness in life.
- I am open to the gentle guidance of the universe.
- I am choosing to focus on my well-being.
- I am open to receiving abundance in all its forms.

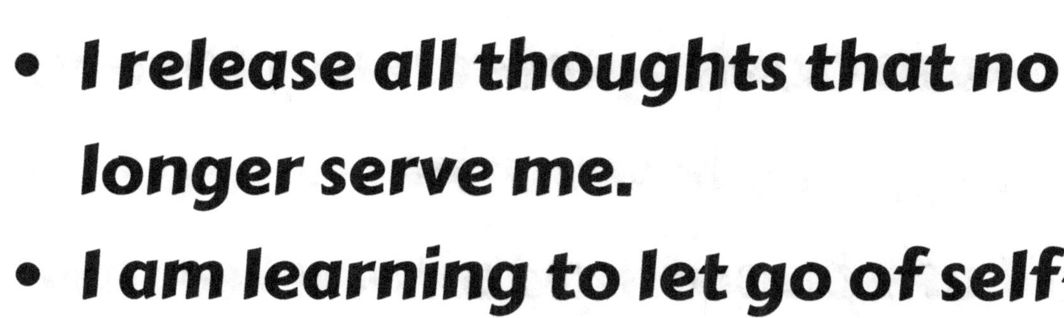

- I release all thoughts that no longer serve me.
- I am learning to let go of self-doubt.
- I am strong, resilient, and adaptable.
- I am deserving of relaxation and peace.
- I am learning to let go of what I cannot control.

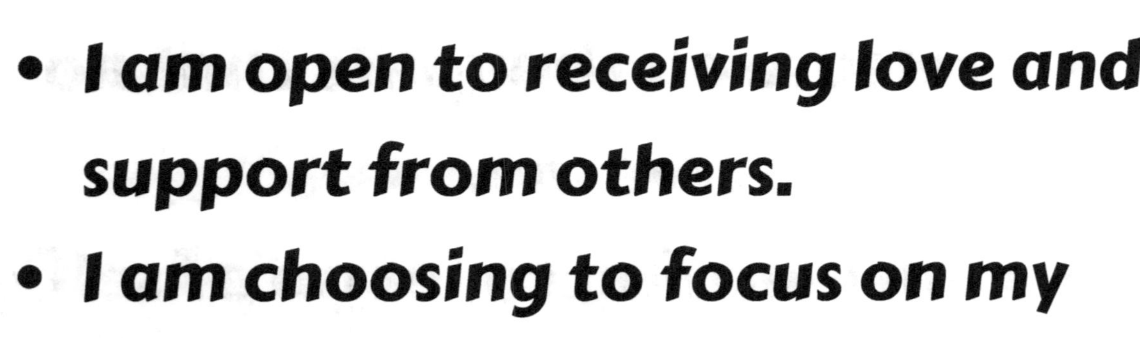

- **I am open to receiving love and support from others.**
- **I am choosing to focus on my inner wisdom.**
- **I release all tension from my body and mind.**
- **I am learning to trust in the timing of life.**
- **I am learning to let go of the need for power.**

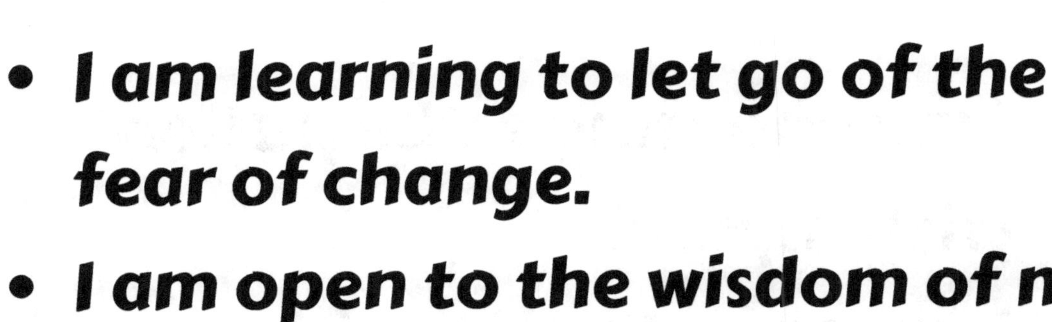

- I am learning to let go of the fear of change.
- I am open to the wisdom of my inner self.
- I am learning to let go of the fear of failure.
- I deserve to feel calm and at ease.
- I am choosing to focus on my strengths.

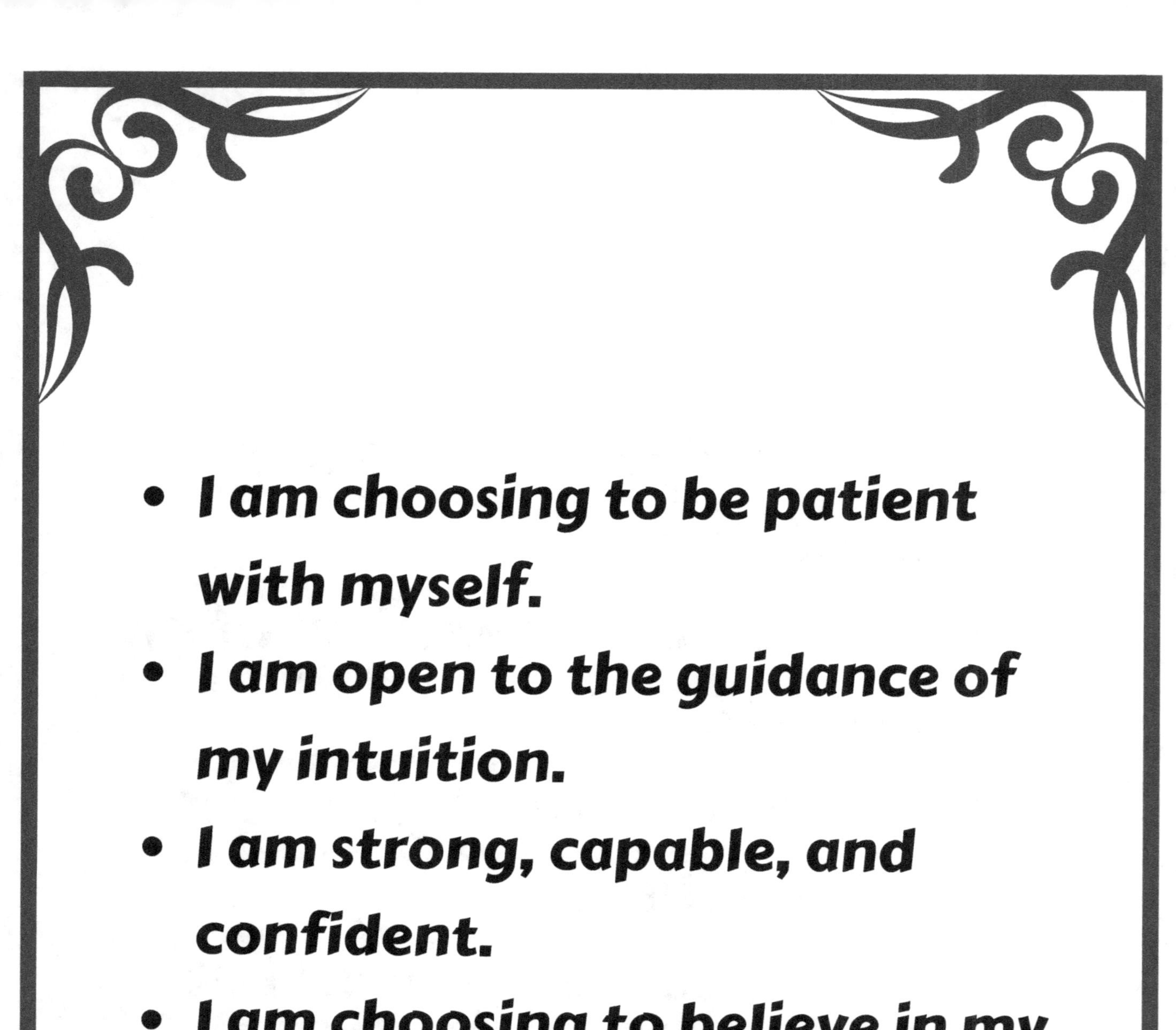

I am choosing to be patient with myself.
I am open to the guidance of my intuition.
I am strong, capable, and confident.
I am choosing to believe in my potential.
I am resilient and adaptable.

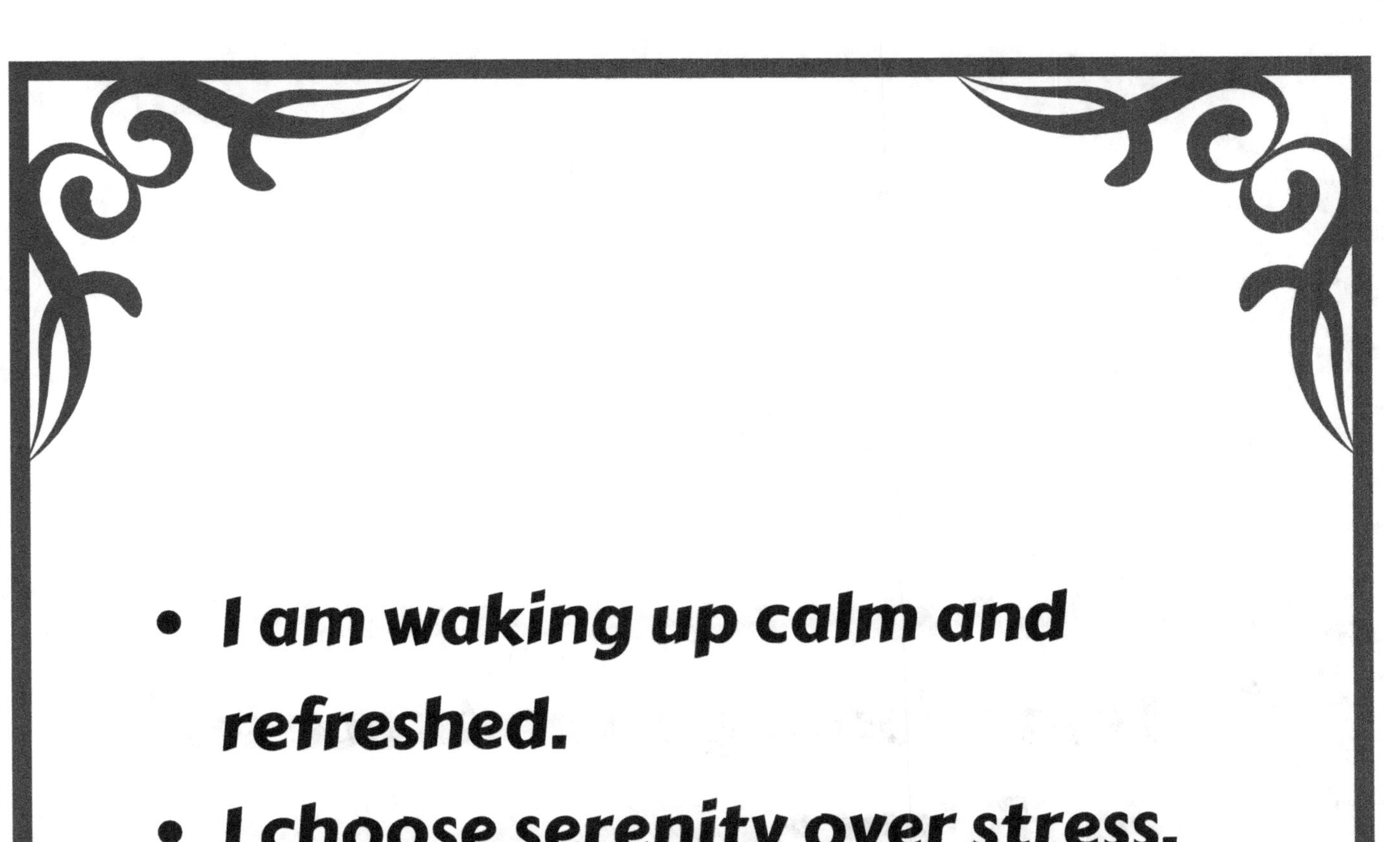

- I am waking up calm and refreshed.
- I choose serenity over stress.
- I am present in the here and now.
- I am releasing the need for perfection.
- I choose peace over worry.

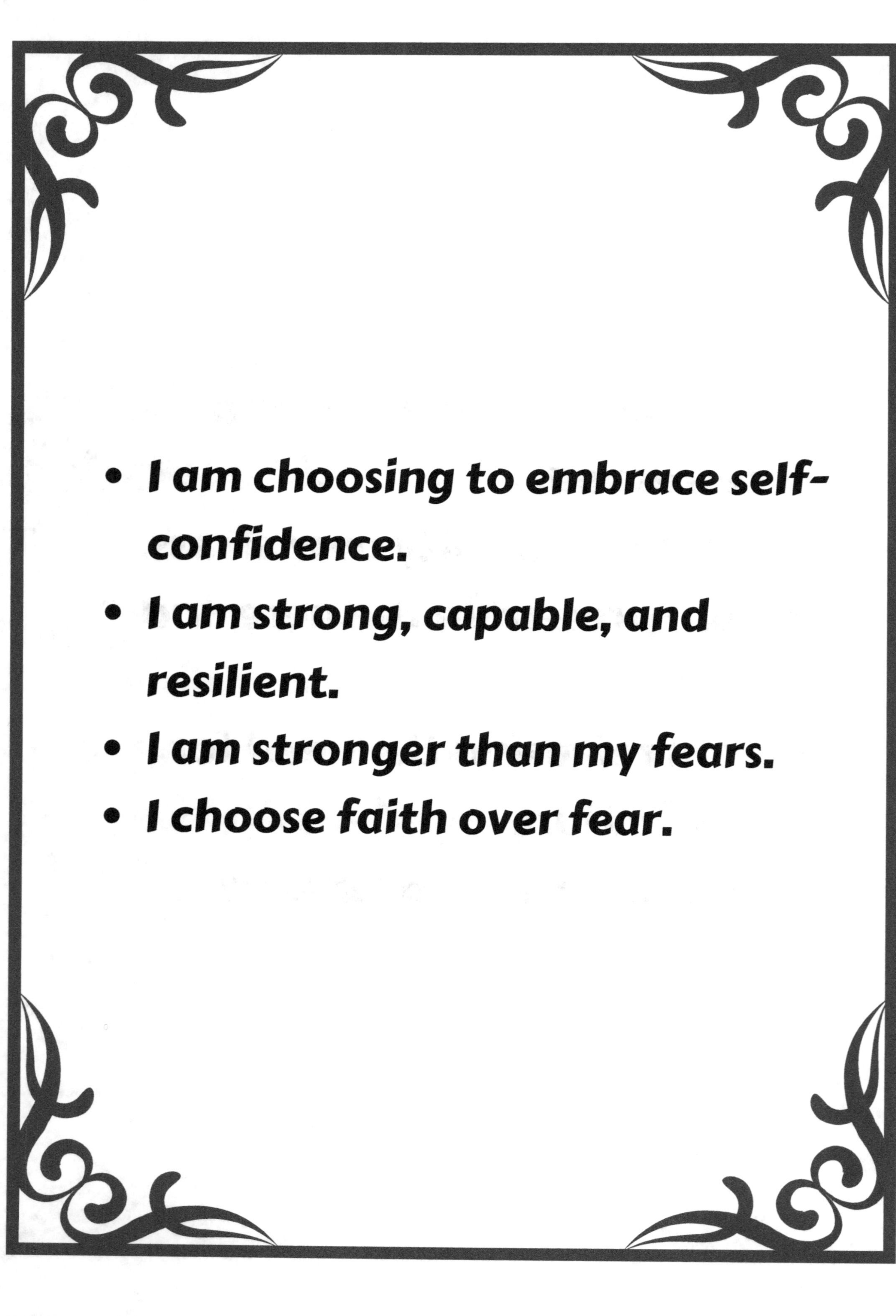

- I am choosing to embrace self-confidence.
- I am strong, capable, and resilient.
- I am stronger than my fears.
- I choose faith over fear.

Notes

Notes